Gifted & Talented®

Science
Questions & Answers

ANIMALS

For Ages 6–8

By Oksana Hlodan

Illustrated by Larry Nolte

LOWELL HOUSE JUVENILE

LOS ANGELES

NTC/Contemporary Publishing Group

To Sarah Kloncz, my wonderful assistant at Habitat for Humanity.
—O.H.

Published by Lowell House
A division of NTC/Contemporary Publishing Group, Inc.
4255 West Touhy Avenue, Lincolnwood (Chicago), Illinois 60646-1975 U.S.A.

Managing Director and Publisher: Jack Artenstein
Director of Publishing Services: Rena Copperman
Editorial Director: Brenda Pope-Ostrow
Director of Art Production: Bret Perry
Editor: Linda Gorman
Designer: Victor W. Perry

Lowell House books can be purchased at special discounts
when ordered in bulk for premiums and special sales.
Please contact Customer Service at:
NTC/Contemporary Publishing Group
4255 W. Touhy Avenue
Lincolnwood, IL 60646-1975
1-800-323-4900

Printed and bound in the United States of America

Library of Congress Catalog Card Number: 98-75624

ISBN: 0-7373-0056-6

10 9 8 7 6 5 4 3 2 1

Note to Parents

Teach a child facts and you give her knowledge. Teach her to think and you give her wisdom. This is the principle behind the entire series of *Gifted & Talented®* materials. And this is the reason that thinking skills are being stressed in classrooms throughout the country.

The questions and answers in the **Gifted & Talented® Question & Answer** books have been designed specifically to promote the development of critical and creative thinking skills. Each page features one "topic question" that is answered above a corresponding picture. This topic provides the springboard to the following questions on the page.

Each of these six related questions focuses on a different higher-level thinking skill. The skills include knowledge and recall, comprehension, deduction, inference, sequencing, prediction, classification, analyzing, problem solving, and creative expansion.

The topic question, answer, and artwork contain the answers or clues to the answers for some of the other questions. Certain questions, however, can only be answered by relating the topic to other facts that your child may already know. At the back of the book are suggested answers to help you guide your child.

Effective questioning has been used to develop a child's intellectual gifts since the time of Socrates. Certainly, it is the most common teaching technique in classrooms today. But asking questions isn't as easy as it looks! On the following page you will find a few tips to keep in mind that will help you and your child use this book more effectively.

★ First of all, let your child flip through the book and select the questions and pictures that interest him or her. If the child wants to do only one page, that's fine. If he or she wants to answer only some of the questions on a page, save the others for another time.

★ Give your child time to think! Wait at least 10 seconds before you offer any help. You'd be surprised how little time many parents and teachers give a child to think before jumping right in and answering a question themselves.

★ Help your child by restating or rephrasing the question if necessary. But again, make sure you pause and give the child time to answer first. Also, don't ask the same question over and over! Go on to another question, or use hints to prompt your child when needed.

★ Encourage your child to give more details or expand upon answers by asking questions such as "What made you say that?" or "Why do you think so?"

★ This book will not only teach your child about many things, but it will teach *you* a lot about your child. Make the most of your time together—and have fun!

The answers at the back of the book are to be used as a guide. Sometimes your child may come up with an answer that is different but still a good answer. Remember, the principle behind all *Gifted & Talented*® materials is to **teach your child to think**—not just to give answers.

What is an insect?

An insect is a small animal with six legs and three main body parts. At the front is the head, with eyes, mouth, and two *antennae* (an-TEH-nay), or feelers. The middle part is the *thorax*. The back part, usually the biggest, is called the *abdomen*. Most insects have wings. Some insects, such as flies and mosquitoes, have two wings. Other insects, such as butterflies and bees, have four wings. All insects hatch from eggs. Scientists have named about one million different *species*, or types, of insects.

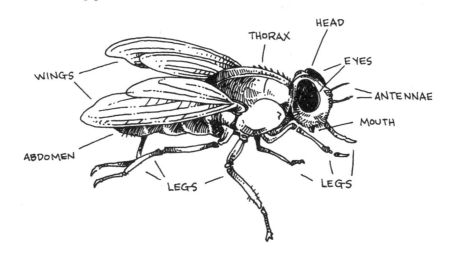

1. How many pairs of legs does an insect have?
2. Do humans have an abdomen? Do humans have antennae?
3. How are a butterfly and a robin alike? How are they different?
4. What are some animals that eat insects?
5. What other animals hatch from eggs?
6. Why do some people think insects are pests?

What is a mammal?

A mammal is an animal that feeds milk to its babies. Mammals are *warm-blooded,* which means their body temperature is always about the same. All mammals have a row of bones down their backs called a *backbone.* Most mammals have hair. Some mammals, such as gorillas, have lots of hair. Other mammals, such as elephants, have very little hair. Mammals also have larger brains than other types of animals. Dogs, cats, horses, pigs, bears, giraffes, and whales are all examples of mammals. Human beings are mammals, too.

1. Why are human beings called mammals?
2. Can you find your backbone? What does it feel like?
3. How does a mother cat feed her kittens?
4. What does **warm-blooded** mean?
5. Can you name some hairy mammals?
6. How do you think having a large brain helps mammals?

What is the fastest animal on land?

The fastest animal on land over short distances is the cheetah. A cheetah is a wildcat that lives in **Africa**. It can run about **60** miles per hour, or about the same speed as a car traveling on a highway. But a cheetah can't run this fast for very long. A cheetah's body is slim and strong, with a long tail for balance. A cheetah digs its sharp claws into the ground and pushes off as it runs. Cheetahs have to be fast so they can catch other animals for food.

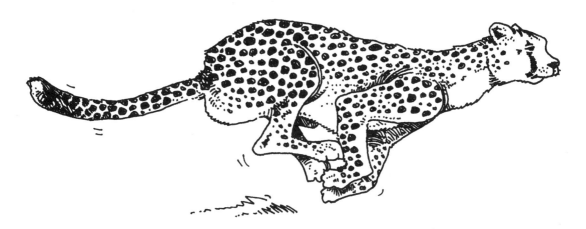

1. What pattern does a cheetah's fur have?
2. Can you name some other animals that run fast?
3. What are some animals that move slowly?
4. What are some other wildcats?
5. At top speed, how far could a cheetah run in one minute?
6. What might happen to a cheetah if it broke a leg?

What is a reptile?

A reptile is a cold-blooded animal, like an insect or a fish. Its blood isn't really cold. *Cold-blooded* means that its body temperature can go up and down, depending on the temperature of its surroundings. On hot days, reptiles stay in the shade to keep cool. On cold days, they lie around in the sunshine to get warm. Reptiles usually have thick and *scaly,* or rough, skin for protection. Most reptiles live on land, but some live in water. Snakes, lizards, crocodiles, and turtles are all reptiles.

1. Why are reptiles called cold-blooded animals?
2. What are some reptiles that live on land?
3. What are some reptiles that live in water?
4. Do you think dinosaurs were reptiles?
5. How is a crocodile's skin different from yours?
6. What things do you do to keep cool on hot days?

How do fish breathe?

When a fish opens its mouth, it takes in water. Water has *oxygen* in it, a gas that almost all living things need in order to survive. When a fish closes its mouth, the water is pumped into its gills, which are located on each side of its head. The gills *absorb,* or take in, the oxygen from the water. The water then flows out of the fish through its gill openings. The gill openings then close, and the breathing process starts all over again.

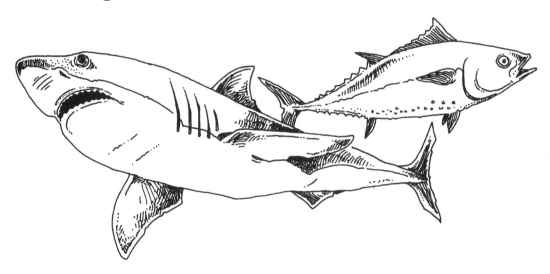

1. How does a fish keep water from entering its gill openings?
2. Why doesn't a fish drown when it swallows water?
3. How do people get oxygen?
4. Why can't fish survive out of water?
5. Why can't people breathe underwater?
6. How do scientists breathe underwater when they study fish?

Why do spiders spin webs?

Spiders spin webs to catch insects to eat. A web is made of threads called *silk*. A spider squeezes the silk out of its body. After making a web, a spider sits on or near the web and waits for an insect to land. Web silk is very sticky, so the insect gets stuck. Quickly, it becomes the spider's meal.

If the spider isn't hungry, it may wrap the insect in silk to eat later. Most spiders inject *venom*, or poison, into a trapped bug to kill it before eating it. Not all spiders spin webs. Some *pounce*, or jump, on their victims from a hiding place.

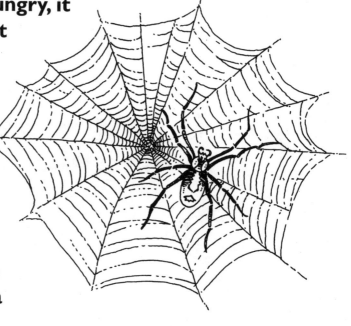

1. Is a spider an insect?
2. How do some spiders that don't spin webs catch food?
3. What would you look for to find out if there's a spider in your house?
4. What are some other things that spin?

5. How is a spider's way of catching food different from a cheetah's way?

6. Why are some people afraid of spiders? Are you?

One Step Further

Make your own cobweb. Put a spool of thread in a small bowl. Pour liquid starch over the spool to cover it completely. Then inflate a balloon or a plastic bag. Hold the balloon or bag over the bowl and wind the wet, sticky thread around it. Keep winding until you have made a cobweb pattern. Cut the end of the thread and smooth it down. Let the thread dry overnight. The next day, pop the balloon or bag and remove it gently from the thread web. Make a spider from some yarn and place it on the web.

How do giraffes use their long necks?

Giraffes stretch their long necks to get at the leaves at the tops of trees. These newer, tastier leaves are their favorite food. This food supply usually doesn't run out because most other animals can't reach that high. To make it even easier to get the leaves, an adult giraffe has a very long tongue. It's almost 21 inches long! Giraffes also use their long necks to look over their surroundings for signs of danger.

1. Why does a giraffe like the leaves at the top of a tree best?
2. Is a giraffe's tongue longer or shorter than a foot?
3. How does a giraffe's long neck help it stay safe?
4. A giraffe is a plant eater, or *herbivore* (ER-bah-vor). Can you name some other herbivores?
5. How is the pattern on a giraffe similar to a puzzle?
6. Would you like to have a long neck like a giraffe? Why or why not?

What is the biggest animal in the ocean?

The blue whale is the biggest animal in the ocean. It is also the largest animal that has ever lived! Even the biggest dinosaur was not as big as the blue whale. An adult blue whale weighs about 300,000 pounds, or as much as about 35 elephants. It measures about 100 feet long, or about the length of five elephants standing one behind the other. Whales are mammals, not fish, and their young are called *calves*. At birth, a blue whale calf is already 23 feet long and weighs about 4,000 pounds!

1. What other baby animals are called *calves*?
2. Can you name some other types of whales? Orca

3. What are some words that rhyme with **whale**?
4. How many feet will a blue whale calf grow to become an adult whale? 300,000
5. How can people in a boat spot a whale in the water? i hole in the back
6. Why do you think people love to watch whales?

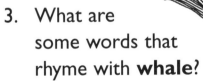
There are nice, there some of them.

How do birds fly?

All birds have feathers. The feathers on a bird's wings and tail are the most important for flying. A bird *steers* itself, or controls its direction, by tilting its wings and twisting its tail. Birds must catch the wind, or *air currents,* to fly. The air currents flow around their feathers, helping them to lift off and fly. The shape of a bird's wings is also important for flight. Wings are slim and have a V shape, which allows air to flow over and under them. Some birds, such as the tiny hummingbird, have to beat their wings a lot to fly. Other birds, such as the eagle, can fly without always beating their wings. They can *glide* through the air. Not all birds can fly. Ostriches and penguins have wings that are not designed for flight.

1. How does a bird change its direction?
2. What animals besides birds can fly?
3. Ducks have waterproof feathers. What does **waterproof** mean?
4. How are airplanes similar to birds?

5. What do you think the expression "Birds of a feather flock together" means?
6. If you could fly like a bird, where would you go?

One Step Further

Experiment with a paper airplane to see how wings work in flight. Follow the instructions and pictures below to create your own airplane from a sheet of paper. Try different wing sizes and a different number of paper clips to see how they change the way the airplane flies.

---

①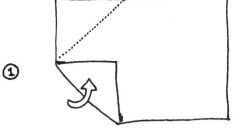

Fold in one corner, then the other.

②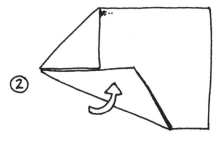

Fold over one wing, then the other.

③

Fold the plane in half.

④

Fold down the wings. Put a paper clip on the nose.

Why do mosquitoes bite?

Mosquitoes don't really bite. We say they bite because when they take our blood, it feels like a bite. Only female mosquitoes "bite." They have a *proboscis* (prah-BOH-sis), which is a long snout shaped like a thin straw. When a female mosquito lands on someone's skin, it pushes its proboscis into the skin to sip blood. Human blood contains material called *protein*. The mosquito needs the protein for its eggs. One mosquito will lay about 100 eggs after drinking a person's blood.

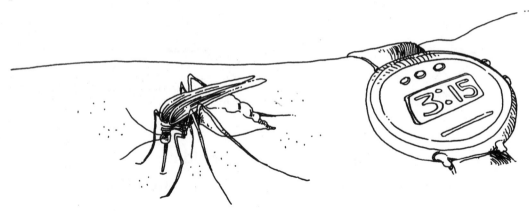

1. How is a proboscis like a straw?
2. Why does a female mosquito want your blood?
3. What kind of animal is a mosquito?
4. How many eggs all together will 10 mosquitoes lay after drinking blood?
5. How do you know when you have been bitten?
6. What can you do to avoid being bitten?

Why can dogs hear sounds that we can't hear?

Dogs hear sounds better than people can because they can move their ears. They can even move one ear at a time. A dog may lift only one of its ears when it picks up a sound. Then it may move its other ear in the same direction. The dog is *capturing* the sound. A dog knows exactly where a sound is coming from in just a few seconds. The design of a dog's ear also allows it to hear certain sounds that people are unable to hear.

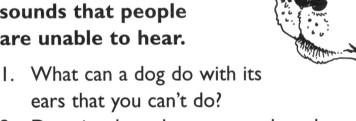

1. What can a dog do with its ears that you can't do?
2. Does it take a dog more or less than a minute to capture a sound?
3. What other strong sense does a dog have?
4. What is a dog whistle?
5. Why are dogs good at protecting homes?
6. How can you change the sound of your voice to tell a dog that it has done something good or bad?

Is a killer whale really a whale?

No, a killer whale is actually a dolphin. Also known as *orcas,* killer whales are the largest of all the dolphins. Dolphins belong to a part of the whale family called *toothed whales* because they have lots of sharp, pointed teeth. Orcas use their sharp teeth to kill prey. Orcas often swim in groups called *pods.* They hunt together in cool waters for squid, fish, seals, and smaller dolphins. They even attack sharks! Although orcas hunt other animals, they are not known to attack people.

1. What is a pod of orcas?
2. Can you think of something else that is called a *pod*?
3. Where could you go to see dolphins?
4. Do you think orcas are afraid of sharks?
5. Should people be afraid of orcas?
6. Why do you think orcas are called "the wolves of the sea"?

Why are there no more dinosaurs?

No one knows for certain why dinosaurs became *extinct*, or died out. But scientists have several *theories*, or ideas. One theory is that the Earth got too cold for dinosaurs, so they died. Another idea is that a huge *asteroid*, or space rock, slammed into the Earth. It created a cloud of dust around the planet, which hid the Sun. Without sunlight, many plants and animals that the dinosaurs ate died, so the dinosaurs died, too. Scientists are hoping that *fossils* will give them more clues. Fossils are bones and other remains of creatures that lived long ago.

1. What does **extinct** mean?
2. What kind of animal was a dinosaur?
3. Where could you go to see fossils?
4. Would you like to dig for fossils? Why or why not?
5. Do you have an idea about why dinosaurs disappeared?
6. Imagine that you have just found the last living dinosaur. What would you do?

How does a chick hatch?

Chicks *develop,* or grow, inside an egg. An egg must be kept warm for a chick to grow. Most birds *incubate* the egg, or keep it warm, by sitting on it. After a chick has developed enough, it breaks out of its egg by cracking the shell. Most chicks have a small, hard bump near their beaks called an egg *tooth.* A chick pecks at the shell with its egg tooth to crack it open. When the egg has cracked open wide enough, the chick wriggles out. Once a chick has hatched, its egg tooth falls off.

1. What does **incubate** mean?
2. How do most birds keep their eggs warm?
3. Where does a bird usually lay its eggs?
4. Eggs in a store are usually sold by the dozen. How many is a dozen?
5. If a bird abandoned its egg, how could you keep the egg warm?
6. What are some other animals that lay eggs?

Why do ants build anthills?

Ants build anthills as they create their nest underground. Ants dig in the ground to create *chambers,* or rooms, that are connected by tunnels. This system of chambers and tunnels is the ants' nest. An anthill is the mound of dirt at the top of the nest. It is made up of the dirt the ants remove from the ground as they tunnel. A group of ants living together is called a *colony.*

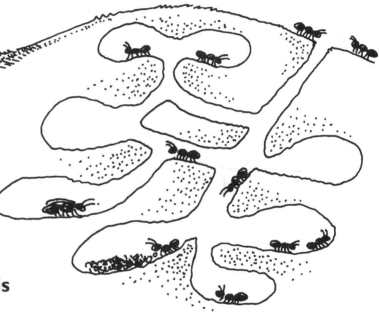

1. What kind of animal is an ant?
2. How is an ants' nest like a city?
3. How can you tell where ants live?
4. What is the difference between an **ant** and an **aunt**?
5. What are some other animals that live underground?
6. Would you like to live underground? Why or why not?

What is an animal family?

A family is a group of animals that have similar *characteristics,* or features. For example, lions, tigers, leopards, and house cats are all members of the cat family. They all have fur, whiskers, tails, and padded feet, they all stalk their prey, and they all tear their food with their claws and teeth. Scientists *classify,* or organize, animals many different ways. The six main *classes* of animals are mammals, reptiles, amphibians, birds, fish, and insects. Within each class are smaller groups called *orders,* and within each order are smaller groups called *families.* For example, a bottle-nosed dolphin is in the dolphin family, in the order called *Cetacea* (sih-TAY-shah), in the class called mammals.

THE CAT FAMILY

1. Who are the members of your family?
2. What are the six major classes of animals?
3. Which class of animals are people in?
4. What rhyming words can you make using the letters in the word **family**?
5. Why do you think scientists organize animals into different groups?
6. Gorillas and human beings are both members of the order called *primates*. How are human beings like gorillas? How are human beings different?

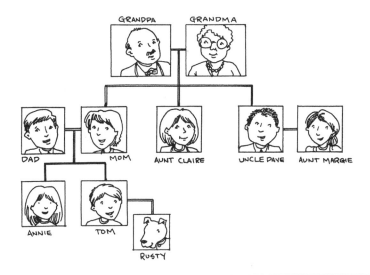

One Step Further

Ask an adult to help you draw your family tree. Write the names of the people in your family on your tree. If you'd like, draw a picture or glue a photo of each person on the tree. Talk about the characteristics your family has in common. For example, do many family members have black hair? Are many of them tall? Can most of them sing well? Make a list of your family traits.

How do bats fly in the dark?

Bats that don't see well in the dark fly by listening for sounds. These bats make squeaking sounds as they fly. When the squeaking sounds hit an object, such as a tree, they bounce back to the bat. A sound that bounces back is called an *echo*. When a bat's big ears hear the echo, it is able to figure out where the object is. This process is called *echolocation*. Bats use echolocation to find insects to eat at night.

1. Why do bats have big ears?
2. Why don't bats fly into trees?
3. What is another meaning for the word **bat**?
4. Bats are called *nocturnal* because they are most active at night. Can you think of some other nocturnal animals?
5. What would happen if you yelled "hello" while standing in a tunnel?
6. Why do you think some people are afraid of bats?

Why do camels have humps?

A camel's hump is mostly made of fat. When a camel can't find food, its body turns the fat in its hump into energy so the camel can survive. Camels live in the desert. Deserts are big, dry places where food and water are sometimes very hard to find. A camel can go for several weeks without eating because it can live off the fat in its hump. *Dromedary* camels have one hump, while *Bactrian* camels have two humps.

1. Why is a camel a good animal for the desert?
2. How long do you think you could go without food?
3. Where is there fat in your body?
4. What happens if you eat more food than your body needs?
5. Why is it hard to find food in the desert?
6. Would you like to live in the desert? Why or why not?

Is coral an animal or a plant?

Although it looks like a plant, coral is actually made up of thousands of tiny animals. These animals, called coral *polyps* (POL-ips), can only live in warm, shallow waters. A place where there is lots of coral is called a *coral reef*. Small fish use the reef to hide from predators. Some corals have hard skeletons on the outside and some are soft.

1. What is a predator?
2. How does a coral reef help small fish?
3. Could coral grow in the Arctic Ocean?
4. Where could you go to see a coral reef?
5. One type of coral is called *brain coral*. How do you think it got its name?
6. Why do you think coral reefs are sometimes called "sea gardens"?

Why do some animals change color?

Some animals change color so they can hide from other animals. For example, the fur of the Arctic fox is white in winter so the fox can blend in with the snow, making it harder to see. In summer, the fox's fur is brown so it can hide more easily in woods and brush. Other animals, such as *chameleons,* a type of lizard, change color if the temperature or light in their environment changes, or if they become frightened. An animal's ability to blend in with its surroundings is called *camouflage* (KA-muh-flahj).

1. Why do some animals turn white in winter?
2. What could you look for to find an Arctic fox in winter?
3. Why does a polar bear's fur stay the same color all year?
4. How is the Arctic fox different from a chameleon?
5. If you were a chameleon, what color would you be right now?
6. Does your skin change color when you are scared? angry? sick?

How do bees make honey?

Bees make honey from a sweet liquid called *nectar* (NEK-tar) that they collect from flowers. Only honeybees and bumblebees make honey. Honeybees live in *hives*, a kind of bee house. Each honeybee in a hive has a specific job. A field bee collects nectar. It sucks up nectar from flowers and stores it in its second stomach, called the *honey stomach*. When it returns to the hive, it gives the nectar to a house bee, who chews on it to make it gooey. The house bee drops the goo into a *cell*, or tiny wax container, inside the hive. The goo sits for a while until it turns into honey.

1. What is a honey stomach?
2. What kind of animal is a bee?
3. What does a beekeeper do?

4. Honey has a sweet taste. What are some other things that taste sweet?
5. Why are some people afraid of bees?
6. What does it mean when we say someone is "as busy as a bee"?

One Step Further

Bees store honey in a *honeycomb*. A honeycomb is made up of many cells. Each cell has six equal sides. A shape with six equal sides is called a *hexagon*. Make a honeycomb pattern using toothpicks and soft candy, such as gumdrops, mini-marshmallows, or jelly beans. Stick toothpicks into the pieces of candy and connect them to make a honeycomb of hexagons.

How do wolves hunt?

Wolves hunt together in a *pack.* A pack is a group of wolves that live together as a family. Wolves are excellent hunters and *prey on,* or attack, large animals such as moose, deer, and elk. A wolf hunting alone would not be able to catch such a large animal. But by working together, a pack can successfully catch large prey. The wolves chase an animal until it is tired, then move in as a group to attack and kill it.

1. What is a baby wolf called?
2. Do you think all the wolves in a pack hunt?
3. What is a lone wolf?
4. What is a werewolf? Do you think werewolves really exist?
5. Do you know any fairy tales that have a wolf in them? What are the names of the stories?
6. Why is it important for people to work together, too?

Why does a rattlesnake rattle its tail?

A rattlesnake, or *rattler* for short, makes a rattling noise to warn other animals when it feels threatened. The rattle is at the tip of a snake's tail and is made of pieces of hard skin called *buttons*. The buttons are stacked on top of each other and are hollow inside. When a rattlesnake shakes its tail, the buttons hit each other and make a buzzing, whirring noise. Rattlesnakes are *venomous*, which means that when they bite, their fangs inject *venom*, or poison, into their victims.

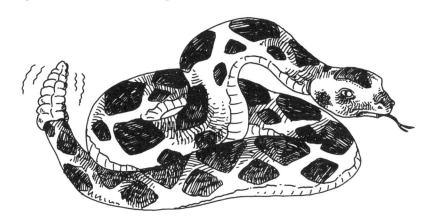

1. What kind of animal is a snake?
2. What other kinds of snakes can you name?
3. How is a baby's toy rattle like a snake's rattle?
4. Why are rattlesnakes dangerous?
5. What sounds do other animals make when they feel threatened?
6. How does a siren act as a warning sound?

Are jellyfish really made of jelly?

No, they're not. Jellyfish got their name because of the soft, jellylike material that makes up their bodies. A jellyfish's body looks soft and wriggly because it doesn't have a skeleton. Most jellyfish swim by opening and shutting their *bell,* the rounded upper part of their bodies. When they stop swimming, they start to sink. As they sink, they trap small animals with their *tentacles,* or arms.

1. How many bones does a jellyfish have?
2. What other sea animals have tentacles?
3. Some jellyfish sting. What other animals can sting?
4. How is a jellyfish's bell like an umbrella?
5. Do you think a jellyfish is a fish?
6. What could happen to a jellyfish if it washed up on a beach?

Do all birds fly?

All birds have wings, but not all birds can fly. Ostriches and penguins are two kinds of birds that are *flightless*, or unable to fly. Their bodies are too big and their wings are too small for them to fly. Instead, ostriches can run very fast and they use their wings for balance. Penguins are excellent swimmers and use their wings like flippers to move themselves through the water.

1. What does **flightless** mean?
2. How do birds that can't fly get from one place to another?
3. Where do ostriches live?
4. Where do penguins live?
5. How does an ostrich's speed help it to survive?
6. Do you think baby birds such as baby eagles and robins can fly? Explain your answer.

How smart are chimpanzees?

Chimpanzees, or *chimps* for short, are very smart. They can solve problems, use tools, and talk to each other. They *communicate,* or talk, by making sounds and using facial expressions. Some scientists have taught chimps to talk to people by using sign language. Sign language is a way of talking with your hands. Chimps are primates, along with human beings and gorillas. Primates have large brains. Scientists believe that larger brains usually mean greater intelligence.

This chimp is making a face that says, "I'm scared."

This chimp is making a face that says, "Let's play."

1. How are you like a chimpanzee?
2. Do you think gorillas are smart? Why or why not?
3. How do people use sign language?
4. Can you say "no," "yes," "I don't know," and "good-bye" without talking? How did you use your body to communicate?
5. What words can you make from the letters in the word **chimpanzee**? Can you make at least 10 words?
6. Why do you think scientists study chimpanzees?

One Step Further

With sign language, you use your fingers to spell. This is how you spell *chimp* using sign language:

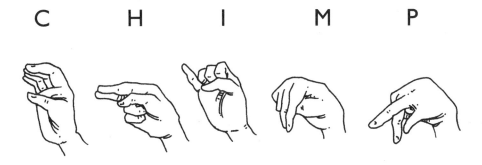

C   H   I   M   P

With a friend or a family member, make up your own finger signs for the letters of the alphabet. Then play a spelling game using your own sign language.

What is the difference between a frog and a toad?

Frogs usually have smooth, slimy skin, but the skin of most toads is bumpy and dry. Frogs have long legs to hop far and jump high. Toads crawl and can only take small hops because their legs are short. Toads are usually wider and flatter than frogs. Frogs and toads belong to the class of animals called *amphibians* (am-FIH-bee-ans). They both live part of their lives in water and part of their lives on land.

1. Which has rougher skin, a frog or a toad?
2. What is a tadpole?
3. How are frogs and toads alike?
4. What other animals live on land and in water?
5. What other animals can jump far?
6. In swimming, there's a style called "the frog." Why do you think it's called that?

Do dragons really exist?

Dragons are only make-believe, but there is a lizard that looks something like a dragon. The *Komodo* (kuh-MOH-doh) dragon is the biggest lizard in the world. It can grow more than 10 feet long and usually weighs about 155 pounds—about as much as a grown person weighs. It has long, sharp claws and jagged teeth. It is very strong and can run very fast. Komodo dragons are *aggressive*, which means they are not afraid to attack. They have even been known to attack and kill people.

1. How is a Komodo dragon like a make-believe dragon?
2. What kind of animal is a lizard?
3. Do you think a Komodo dragon would make a good pet? Why or why not?
4. How much do you weigh? How much more than you does a full-grown Komodo dragon weigh?
5. What other make-believe animals have you heard stories about?
6. Can you make up a story about a friendly dragon? Tell your story to a friend.

Why do squirrels bury nuts?

Squirrels bury nuts and other food in the ground or under leaves to prepare for winter. Squirrels love to eat nuts, seeds, and acorns. It's hard for them to find these foods in winter. So they hide as much food as they can in summer and fall. A squirrel's good memory and strong sense of smell allow it to find the food months after it has been hidden. But some nuts never get eaten. These buried nuts may eventually grow into trees.

1. When do squirrels eat the food they have hidden?
2. How do squirrels find the hidden food?
3. What kinds of nuts can you name?
4. How do squirrels help forests?
5. What do some other animals do when winter comes?
6. What are some good hiding places in your home? Do you ever hide things?

How does snow help penguins?

Snow and ice help penguins move around on land. Penguins move best in water. They are great swimmers, using their small wings like flippers. But out of water, penguins have to walk because they are too heavy to fly. Their legs are short, so they waddle when they walk. If there is ice or snow around, some penguins travel by sliding along on their bellies. This allows them to move faster and is called *tobogganing*.

1. Where do penguins move best?
2. Why can't penguins fly?
3. What does **waddle** mean?
4. What is a toboggan?
5. What other animals live where penguins live?
6. What are some things people do when there's snow?

How does a caterpillar become a butterfly?

Some insects can change the look of their bodies. This change is called *metamorphosis* (meh-tah-MOR-fah-sis). A butterfly changes in four steps. First, it is born as a tiny egg. Then a caterpillar hatches from the egg. During the next few weeks, the caterpillar eats and grows a lot. When the caterpillar is full grown, it changes into a *pupa* (**PYOO**-pah). Inside the hard-shelled pupa, many physical changes take place. The pupal stage can last several days or more than a year. Finally, the pupa splits open and a beautiful butterfly emerges from the shell.

The Life Cycle of a Monarch Butterfly

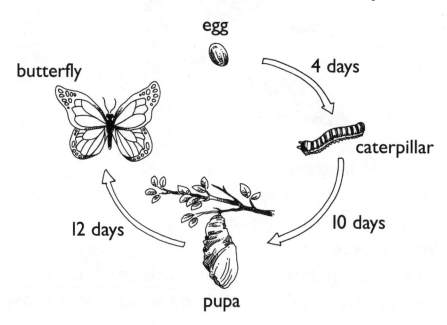

1. How many days does metamorphosis take for a monarch butterfly?
2. How do a butterfly's colors protect it from its enemies?
3. Monarch butterflies migrate during the winter. What does this mean?
4. How have you changed since you were a baby?
5. If you could spin a cocoon and change into an animal, what animal would you want to be? Why?
6. Why do you think some people collect butterflies?

One Step Further

You can study an insect's life cycle, from birth to death, at home. Put a little meat, sugar, and food scraps in a glass jar. Catch a few flies and put them in the jar. Cover the lid with cheesecloth or other material that lets air into the jar. Put a rubber band around the top of the jar to hold the cloth in place. Watch what happens for the next 21 days. Release the flies outside when your experiment is finished.

How does an elephant use its trunk?

An elephant uses its trunk to breathe and smell. It also uses it to bring food and water up to its mouth. Sometimes an elephant uses its trunk like a hand. The trunk is very strong and can pick up a fallen tree weighing 600 pounds. The trunk is also very flexible and can easily curve around a ball. When it's hot, an elephant uses its trunk as a water hose to stay cool. It sucks water into its trunk and sprays the water over its body.

1. What part of your body do you use to breathe and smell?

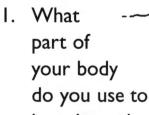

2. What is a baby elephant called?
3. Can you think of other meanings for the word **trunk**?
4. Do you think an elephant is afraid of other animals?
5. How could an elephant use its trunk to defend itself?
6. What things do you do to stay cool when it's hot?

Do mice really like cheese?

Mice will eat cheese, but they prefer other kinds of food. They eat bread, cereal, nuts, and seeds. They also seem to like chocolate. When mice are very hungry, they will eat anything, even glue or soap. Mice *forage,* or search for food, outside, but if they can get into a building, they will go in to search for an easier meal. People who manage grocery stores think mice are pests because they chew on containers to get to the food inside.

1. What foods do you like to eat?
2. Why shouldn't people eat glue or soap?
3. What is a pest?
4. Why are mice afraid of cats?
5. How does a mouse's sharp front teeth help it to survive?
6. What are some signs that there is a mouse in your home?

Why does an owl have big eyes?

An owl has big eyes so it can see well in the dark. Owls are *nocturnal,* which means they are most active at night. Unlike people, owls can't move their eyes. To watch a moving object, an owl has to turn its whole head. An owl's neck allows the head to turn almost all the way around. Sometimes it looks like an owl has eyes on the back of its head! Some people think that an owl's large eyes make it look wise.

1. Have you ever heard an owl? What sound does an owl make?
2. When does an owl hunt for food?
3. What other animals are active at night?
4. What does **wise** mean?
5. What does someone mean if he or she says "I don't give a hoot!"?
6. Make up a story about a wise owl that the forest animals come to for help. What problems do the animals have? What advice does the owl give them?

Why do turtles have shells?

Turtles have shells for protection. Most turtles can pull their heads, legs, and tails into their shells when they feel threatened. The shell is very hard, like a suit of armor. It has a pattern like a jigsaw puzzle. Most turtle shells are black, brown, or dark green, but some have brighter colors on them. A turtle can't leave its shell because parts of its body are attached to it.

1. Does a turtle always travel with its shell?
2. What kind of animal is a turtle?
3. Why do we sometimes say that someone is "as slow as a turtle"?
4. What is a tortoise?
5. How is a turtle like a crab? How is it different?
6. Would you like to have a shell like a turtle? Draw a picture of what you would look like if you had a shell.

Why do tigers have stripes?

Tigers have dark stripes to help them blend in with their natural *environment,* or surroundings. This makes them hard to see. A tiger hides in bushes and tall grass when it hunts. Another animal passing by may not see it. The tiger can then pounce on the animal from its hiding place. When an animal has colors or a pattern that blends in with its surroundings, we call it *camouflage* (KA-muh-flahj). Every tiger has a *unique* pattern of stripes on its coat, which means each pattern is different.

1. What does **pounce** mean?
2. A tiger is one of the *big cats.* Can you name some other big cats?
3. What other animals have interesting patterns on their fur or skin?
4. Can you think of some other things that are unique, or one of a kind?
5. Can a cow camouflage itself? Why or why not?
6. What clothes would you wear if you wanted to hide in a forest? in the snow?

What is a school of fish?

A *school* is a group of fish that live together. Different fish swim together in different *formations,* or shapes. Herring swim together in the shape of a wavy ribbon. Sardines form a ball when they are frightened. Fish swim in schools because it's safer than swimming alone. Not all fish swim in schools. *Predators,* or hunters, such as sharks, usually swim alone.

1. Do all schools of fish swim together in the same way?
2. Why do you think sharks swim alone?
3. Other kinds of animals also live in groups. What is a group of lions called? a group of wolves? a group of birds?
4. Why should a person never swim alone?
5. When do you like to be with a group of people?
6. When do you like to be alone?

Why do frogs croak?

A frog croaks, squeaks, and whistles to *communicate,* or talk, to other frogs. The sounds a frog makes tell other frogs where it is, how big it is, and what kind of frog it is. Male frogs also croak loudly to attract female frogs. A frog has a special *sac,* or pouch, on its throat. When the frog breathes air in, the sac fills up with air. When it breathes air out, it makes a croaking sound.

1. How is a frog's sac similar to a balloon?
2. What kind of animal is a frog?
3. What animal looks a lot like a frog but lives mostly on land?
4. Where does the air go when you breathe in?
5. What does it mean to have "a frog in your throat"?
6. Where could you go to study frogs?

How does a rabbit hop?

A rabbit hops by pushing off from the ground with its powerful *hind,* or back, legs. A rabbit's hind legs are longer than its front legs. The hind legs have strong muscles that help the rabbit hop high and far. A rabbit can travel as far as 10 feet with just one hop. Rabbits also use their hind legs to thump the ground. The thumping sound warns other rabbits when danger is near.

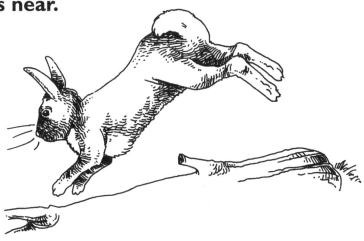

1. What other animals can hop?
2. How far could a rabbit travel in five hops?
3. What are some things that rabbits like to eat?
4. Do you think a rabbit would make a good pet? Why or why not?
5. Can you think of some famous rabbits from books, movies, cartoons, or nursery rhymes?
6. What are some ways that people warn other people about danger?

Why do beavers build dams?

Beavers build dams to block streams. A beaver dam is a kind of wall made up of branches, logs, rocks, and mud. A dam built across a stream blocks the flow of the water. This raises the level of the water behind the dam and creates a pond. Beavers then build a lodge, or home, at the pond. All the entrances to the lodge are underwater so that the beavers' enemies can't get in. The beavers check the entrances often to make sure that they stay underwater. If the water level gets too low, the beavers will build a second dam or make the first one bigger.

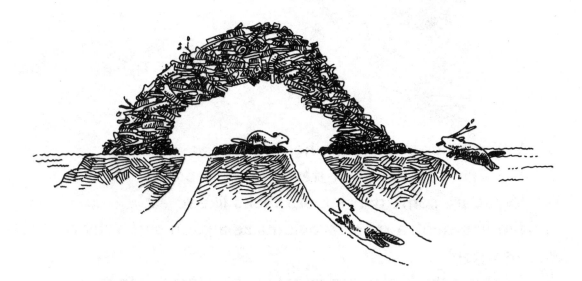

1. What is the difference between a beaver dam and a beaver lodge?
2. Why do you think beavers have big front teeth?

3. Why do beavers have to be good swimmers?
4. What does "busy as a beaver" mean?
5. What country is the beaver a symbol for?
6. Why do some people think beaver dams are a problem?

One Step Further

Find out how a beaver stays warm in winter. With an adult's help, fill four glass jars with hot water. Measure the temperature of the water in each jar with a thermometer. Then put the lids on the jars. Put one jar in the middle of a cardboard box. Fill the empty space around the jar with solid material, such as packing chips or popcorn. Wrap the second jar in a handkerchief. Wrap the third jar in a wool scarf. Don't wrap the last jar. Measure the temperature of each jar every half hour and write down your observations. Which jar stays the warmest? Which jar cools down the fastest? Can you explain your results?

Why do woodpeckers peck on trees?

Woodpeckers *peck,* or drill, holes in trees to search for food. They eat the insects that live inside trees. A woodpecker's beak is long and pointy, perfect for drilling holes into wood. When a woodpecker finds an insect inside a hole, it gets the insect out with its long, sticky tongue. Woodpeckers also peck holes in trees to make nests. If a woodpecker can't find a hole in a tree big enough for a nest, it will drill one out with its beak.

1. How does a woodpecker's tongue help it to get food?
2. Where does a woodpecker lay its eggs?
3. How does a woodpecker cling to a tree as it pecks?
4. What animals besides birds live in trees?
5. What words can you make using the letters in the word **woodpecker**? Can you make at least 10 words?
6. A woodpecker is a bird that pecks on wood. What other animals have names that describe what they do?

Do sharks ever lose their teeth?

Yes, sharks lose their teeth often, but the lost teeth are replaced by new ones. A shark has several rows of teeth in its mouth. When a tooth breaks off in the front row, another tooth moves forward from the row behind it. A lost tooth can be replaced in as little as eight days. In its lifetime, a shark can have thousands of teeth and lose just as many.

1. Why are people afraid of sharks? Are you afraid of them?
2. Why do people sometimes find shark's teeth on a beach?
3. What happens when a young child loses a tooth?
4. What happens when an adult loses a tooth?
5. What should you do to take good care of your teeth?
6. What are some other things that are set in rows?

What do koalas eat?

Koalas eat the leaves of *eucalyptus* (yoo-kah-LIP-tus) trees. A koala spends almost all of its time in trees, sleeping. It sleeps up to 18 hours a day! The rest of the time, it eats leaves. A koala uses its large teeth to bite off the long, tough eucalyptus leaves. Then it grinds them into a paste before swallowing. An adult koala eats about 2 pounds of leaves every day. Both koalas and eucalyptus trees are *native* to Australia, which means they both come from there.

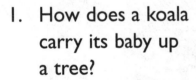

1. How does a koala carry its baby up a tree?
2. What is a baby koala called?
3. How many hours a day do you sleep? How many more hours a day does a koala sleep than you?
4. Where is Australia? Can you find it on a map or a globe?
5. What are some other animals that live in Australia?
6. Do you think you would like to eat one kind of food all the time? Why or why not?

How can a snake swallow big things?

A snake can swallow big things because its jawbones are loosely attached. When a snake opens its mouth, the bones in its jaw spread wide apart. The left and right sides of its jaw can also be moved separately. These movements allow a snake to swallow an animal that is even bigger than the snake's head. Snakes eat small animals, such as birds, frogs, lizards, and mice. A snake swallows an animal whole, without chewing it or biting off small pieces.

1. What ways can you move your jaw?
2. Why does a snake need to be able to open its mouth wide?
3. Have you ever touched a snake? What did it feel like?
4. Why do you think some people are afraid of snakes? Are you?
5. Why is it dangerous for a person to swallow food without chewing it?
6. There is a river in the United States called the Snake River. How do you think it got its name?

Why is a hippopotamus so lazy?

A hippopotamus, or *hippo* for short, is not really lazy. It just looks lazy because it spends most of each day resting in water. Hippos are very heavy. Being in water makes them feel lighter because water makes things more *buoyant,* or able to float. Resting in water also keeps a hippo cool. A hippo's eyes, ears, and nostrils are high on its head, which lets the hippo see, hear, and breathe even when it is almost completely underwater. Hippos come out on land at night to feed.

1. What are nostrils?
2. Why is it important for a hippo's nostrils to stay above water?
3. How does your body feel when you're in water?
4. Do you ever feel lazy? What do you do when you're feeling lazy?
5. Why do you think hippos come out on land mostly at night?
6. Only two land animals are bigger than a hippopotamus. Can you name them?

Why do fireflies glow?

Fireflies have organs in their *abdomen,* or stomach, that have chemicals that light up. Everything in the world is made up of chemicals. For example, air has the chemical *oxygen.* Fireflies don't glow constantly, like a lamp. Instead, they blink on and off. Scientists think fireflies blink to signal each other. Some groups of fireflies blink all together at the same time.

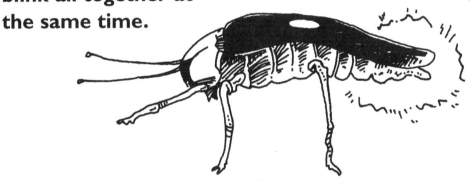

1. When is the best time of day to see fireflies?
2. What are some other things that blink?
3. Why do you think fireflies are also called *lightning bugs*?
4. How is a firefly like a lighthouse?
5. **Firefly** is a compound word. Compound words are made up of two smaller words. Can you think of some more compound words that have the word **fire** in them?
6. What might happen to a firefly if it stopped glowing? Make up a story and tell it to a friend or a family member.

Why do ducks have webbed feet?

Ducks have webbed feet so that they can swim better. A *web* is the skin that joins the three front toes on a duck's foot. The back toe is not attached to the web. The web creates a surface that is flat and wide, like the end of a boat paddle. A duck can easily scoot around in the water by paddling with its webbed feet.

1. How many toes does a duck have in all?
2. What other animals have webbed feet?
3. How would a duck paddle to the left or to the right?
4. Why does a duck waddle when it's on land?
5. Why do you think skin divers wear flippers?
6. Why don't people have webbed feet?

Why does an octopus squirt ink?

An octopus squirts ink to hide itself. The dark-colored ink comes from an ink sac inside the large main part of an octopus's body. When an octopus feels threatened by *predators,* animals that want to attack it, it sprays out ink. The ink forms a dark cloud in the water. This makes it hard to see the octopus. The inky cloud doesn't *disperse,* or break up, right away. This gives the octopus time to escape from the danger.

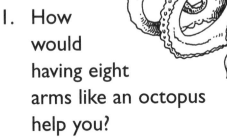

1. How would having eight arms like an octopus help you?
2. How would having eight arms be a problem?
3. Why do you think octopuses have suckers under their arms?
4. How is an octopus like a skunk?
5. What does it mean when a crowd of people disperses?
6. When you get scared, what do you do to make yourself feel safe?

Answers

PAGE 5
1. Three.
2. Humans have an abdomen but do not have antennae.
3. They are alike because they both have wings and can fly. They are different because a butterfly is an insect and has four wings, while a robin is a bird and has two wings.
4. Sample answers: Birds, fish, anteaters, spiders, bats, and frogs.
5. Sample answers: Birds, fish, turtles, frogs, and snakes.
6. Sample answers: Because insects sting us, infect us with diseases, attack crops, get into our food, and damage property.

PAGE 6
1. Because we feed milk to our babies, have hair, are warm-blooded, and have a backbone.
2. It feels like a series of bumps down the back from the neck to the waist.
3. Kittens drink milk from the nipples on the mother cat's belly.
4. It means that the temperature of the body is usually the same and that the temperature is controlled by the body, not by the environment.
5. Sample answers: Monkeys, sheep, cats, dogs, bears, lions, and tigers.
6. Having a large brain allows mammals to think, not just rely on their instincts. Mammals such as humans, apes, dolphins, and elephants are highly intelligent.

PAGE 7
1. It has spotted fur.
2. Sample answers: Horses, gazelles, jackrabbits, ostriches, roadrunners, and greyhounds.
3. Sample answers: Turtles, snails, sloths, and worms.
4. Sample answers: Lions, tigers, leopards, and jaguars.
5. I mile.
6. It would not be able to chase and catch animals for food, and so might not survive.

PAGE 8
1. Their body temperature changes according to their surroundings.
2. Sample answers: Most snakes and lizards, and tortoises.

3. Sample answers: Crocodiles, alligators, turtles, and some snakes.
4. Dinosaurs were the largest reptiles that ever lived.
5. A crocodile has thick, rough skin, but a person has soft, thin skin.
6. Sample answers: Drink cool liquids, wear light clothing and a hat, stay in the shade, and go swimming.

PAGE 9
1. It closes them.
2. It gets rid of the water through its gills.
3. By breathing air.
4. Because their bodies are not designed to get oxygen from the air. They can only get oxygen from water.
5. People do not have gills, so they can't get oxygen from the water.
6. They wear a tank on their backs that contains air and breathe the air through a special hose and mouthpiece.

PAGES 10–11
1. No, a spider is an arachnid. It has eight legs and two body parts. Insects have six legs and three body parts.
2. Some spiders pounce on insects, sometimes injecting venom, or poison, into their prey.
3. Cobwebs.
4. Sample answers: A top, a dryer, a propeller, and a compact disc.
5. A spider builds a trap to catch food and a cheetah chases its prey.
6. Answers will vary.

PAGE 12
1. Because they are newer and tastier than the other leaves.
2. Almost 9 inches longer.
3. Because its head is so high, a giraffe can spot danger sooner than shorter animals can.
4. Sample answers: Cows, horses, sheep, rabbits, deer, elephants, and zebras.
5. The brown patches fit together sort of like the way the pieces of a jigsaw puzzle fit together.
6. Answers will vary.

PAGE 13
1. Baby cows and baby elephants.
2. Sample answers: Humpback, sperm, gray, beluga, and killer whales.
3. Sample answers: Snail, trail, pail, jail, mail, nail, sail, tail, sale, and tale.

4. About 77 feet.
5. By looking for a whale's *spout*. A spout is a misty-looking cloud of air and water vapor that a whale blows out of its blowhole when it exhales.
6. Answers will vary.

PAGES 14–15
1. It tilts its wings and twists its tail.
2. Sample answers: Bees, flies, butterflies, moths, and bats.
3. It means that the feathers don't let water get through to the duck's skin.
4. Airplanes are designed like birds so they can fly. Most have wings and a tail.
5. It means that people who are alike or who share similar interests often spend time together and become friends.
6. Answers will vary.
One Step Further: The size of the wings will affect how high and how far the plane flies. More paper clips will add weight, allowing the plane to fly straighter.

PAGE 16
1. It is long and hollow, and liquid is sucked through it.
2. To help its eggs develop.
3. An insect.
4. 1000 eggs.
5. There will be a tiny red bump on the skin that usually itches.
6. Sample answers: Wear clothes that cover the arms and legs, use bug repellent, and stay away from swampy or wet areas.

PAGE 17
1. It can move its ears, one at a time.
2. Less than a minute. A dog can capture a sound in just a few seconds.
3. An excellent sense of smell.
4. A whistle that dogs can hear but humans can't.
5. Because they can hear faint noises made by an intruder.
6. If you speak with a soft or pleasant voice, the dog knows that it's been good. If you raise your voice or speak harshly, it tells the dog that it's done something naughty.

PAGE 18
1. A group of orcas that live and hunt together.
2. A pea pod.

3. Sample answers: Aquariums, marine parks, and in the open ocean on tour boats.
4. No. They sometimes attack sharks.
5. No. Orcas are not known to attack people.
6. Because they hunt together in a group like wolves do.

PAGE 19
1. It means something no longer exists.
2. A reptile.
3. A museum.
4–6. Answers will vary.

PAGE 20
1. It means to keep an egg warm so it can hatch.
2. By sitting on them.
3. In a nest.
4. A dozen means 12.
5. By putting it on a warm blanket and shining a light on it.
6. Sample answers: Insects, frogs, snakes, alligators, and some fish.

PAGE 21
1. An insect.
2. It has roads (tunnels) and living spaces (chambers).
3. You can see the mound of earth created by their digging.
4. An *ant* is a small insect. An *aunt* is the sister of a person's mother or father.
5. Sample answers: Worms, moles, woodchucks, gophers, and some mice.
6. Answers will vary.

PAGES 22–23
1. Answers will vary.
2. Mammals, reptiles, amphibians, birds, fish, and insects.
3. Mammals.
4. Sample answers: Am and yam; lay and may; mail and fail.
5. Scientists have named more than a million and a half species of animals. Organizing them into smaller groups makes it easier to study them and understand them.
6. Gorillas and human beings are alike because they have similar skeletons, are very intelligent, can hold objects with their hands, and have nails instead of claws. They are different because a gorilla has thick hair all over its body, its arms are longer than its legs, it usually walks on all fours, and it cannot talk.
One Step Further: Draw a family tree, identifying as many members of the family as you can and listing things they have in common.

PAGE 24
1. So they can hear sounds better.

2. The squeaks the bat makes bounce off trees and back to the bat, which lets the bat know where the trees are.
3. A wooden or aluminum stick used to hit a ball in baseball.
4. Sample answers: Owls, skunks, raccoons, and coyotes.
5. The sound would bounce off the walls of the tunnel and create an echo. The echo would repeat the word *hello*.
6. Answers will vary.

PAGE 25
1. Because a camel can go for long periods without food or water, which can be hard to find in the desert.
2. Answers will vary.
3. Under your skin.
4. The extra food turns into fat.
5. Because the desert is very dry and few plants can grow there.
6. Answers will vary.

PAGE 26
1. An animal that chases and eats other animals for food.
2. It provides a place for them to hide from predators.
3. No. Coral can only survive in warm, tropical water.
4. Reefs can be found in different parts of the world where there is warm, shallow water. Reefs exist along the coasts of Florida, Australia, and Brazil, and throughout the South Pacific.
5. Brain coral has ridges and grooves and a rounded shape, and looks similar to the human brain.
6. Because the coral has bright colors in many different shapes, like the brightly colored flowers in a garden.

PAGE 27
1. Because snow is white and having white fur makes the animals less visible.
2. You could look for paw prints in the snow.
3. Polar bears have no natural enemies, so they have less need to hide or blend in with their surroundings.
4. An Arctic fox changes color as the seasons change. A chameleon changes color as its environment changes or when it becomes afraid.
5. Answers will vary.
6. Most people's faces turn pink or red when they're angry and pale when they're scared or sick.

PAGES 28–29
1. It is a field bee's second stomach and the place where it stores the nectar it collects.

2. An insect.
3. A beekeeper keeps many hives of bees, collects the honey the bees make, and sells it.
4. Sample answers: Sugar, candy, chocolate, cake, and cookies.
5. Because bees sometimes sting people. Bee stings are painful and can make some people very sick.
6. It means the person is very busy and working very hard.

PAGE 30
1. A pup.
2. No. Young wolf pups stay behind in a sheltered place while the older wolves hunt.
3. A wolf that has left its pack and travels alone.
4. According to legend, a werewolf is a person who turns into a wolf. Rest of answer will vary.
5. Sample answers: *The Three Little Pigs* and *Little Red Riding Hood.*
6. By working together, people help each other get things done. They also can do more things than one person alone could do.

PAGE 31
1. A reptile.
2. Sample answers: Pythons, boa constrictors, cobras, garter snakes, copperheads, and vipers.
3. Both make a buzzing sound when they're shaken.
4. Because their fangs inject venom into their victims when they bite, and this venom can be deadly.
5. Sample answers: Dogs growl, cats hiss, birds screech, elephants trumpet, and tigers snarl.
6. A siren on an ambulance, a fire truck, or a police car lets people know that the vehicle is coming so that they can get off the road or move to the side to let it pass.

PAGE 32
1. None. It has no skeleton.
2. Sample answers: Octopuses and squid.
3. Sample answers: Bees and wasps.
4. They both have a rounded shape, and can open wide and close tight.
5. No. Fish are *vertebrates,* which means they have a backbone, but a jellyfish has no skeleton.
6. It would die unless a wave pulled it back into the water.

PAGE 33
1. It means "not able to fly."
2. They walk, run, or swim.
3. In Africa.

4. Penguins can be found in Antarctica, Australia, New Zealand, South America, and the Galapagos Islands. They only live south of the equator.
5. Its speed helps it run away from its enemies, such as lions and cheetahs.
6. No, baby birds can't fly. Most are born blind, have almost no feathers, and are very weak.

PAGES 34–35

1. Both people and chimpanzees are primates with large brains, are intelligent, use tools, and communicate with their own kind.
2. Gorillas are very intelligent. They are primates and have large brains.
3. People who are deaf or who can't speak use sign language to communicate.
4. You can say "no" by shaking your head, "yes" by nodding your head, "I don't know" by shrugging your shoulders, and "good-bye" by waving your hand.
5. Many words can be made. Sample answers: Man, mane, maze, pan, can, cane, hen, ham, zip, chip, chin, pin, name, cape, pea, and peach.
6. Because chimpanzees are intelligent, they are physically very similar to humans, and the way chimps behave and act toward each other is similar to the way humans behave.

PAGE 36

1. A toad.
2. A baby frog or toad.
3. Both are amphibians and live part of their lives on land and part in water. Both are born from eggs laid in water. Both have long, sticky tongues that they use to catch prey such as insects.
4. Sample answers: Turtles, crocodiles, alligators, seals, penguins, and hippopotamuses.
5. Sample answers: Rabbits, hares, and kangaroos.
6. Because the motion of a swimmer's arms and legs while swimming in that style looks similar to the way a frog swims.

PAGE 37

1. Both are very big and dangerous, with lots of sharp claws and jagged teeth. Both creatures look like some kind of dinosaur.
2. A reptile.
3. No, a Komodo dragon is too dangerous to be a safe pet.
4–6. Answers will vary.

PAGE 38

1. During the winter.
2. They use their strong sense of smell

and good memory to find it.
3. Sample answers: Peanuts, almonds, walnuts, pecans, hazelnuts, and cashews.
4. They bury nuts in the ground. If they do not eat the nuts, the nuts may grow into new trees and help keep the forest healthy.
5. Some animals hibernate and some animals migrate to warmer places.
6. Answers will vary.

PAGE 39

1. In the water.
2. Because their wings are too small and their bodies are too heavy.
3. It means to walk with short steps, with the body swaying from side to side.
4. A long, flat sled that is curled at one end, used for sliding on snow.
5. Sample answers: Leopard seals, elephant seals, killer whales, sperm whales, blue whales, terns, and albatrosses.
6. Sample answers: Go skiing, go snowshoeing, build a snowman, or go tobogganing.

PAGES 40–41

1. 26 days.
2. Most butterflies look like their surroundings, such as flowers or bushes, so that they can hide from their enemies. But some butterflies, like the monarch, stand out on purpose, to warn other animals that they are not good to eat.
3. It means that they fly to warmer places.
4. Sample answers: You are much taller, you weigh more, you can talk and walk, you can feed and dress yourself, and you eat different foods.
5–6. Answers will vary.
One Step Further: You will see eggs hatch into newborn flies.

PAGE 42

1. Your nose.
2. A calf.
3. Sample answers: A trunk can be the main stem of a tree, a large storage box, or the storage compartment of a car.
4. Lions and tigers sometimes attack calves, but grown elephants have few enemies.
5. An elephant could use its trunk like a club to hit an animal.
6. Sample answers: Go swimming, stay indoors with air conditioning, wear light clothes, drink cold liquids, and eat ice cream.

PAGE 43

1. Answers will vary.
2. Because they can make people very sick.

3. Something that is annoying or bothersome.
4. Because cats hunt mice and are excellent hunters.
5. The teeth can chew through cardboard, cloth, and wood, which allows the mouse to get at whatever food may be inside.
6. Sample answers: Holes in boxes or bags of food; chew marks on plants, books, or furniture; small holes in walls; and scurrying sounds between walls.

PAGE 44

1. An owl makes a "whoo, whoo, whoo" sound.
2. At night.
3. Sample answers: Bats, raccoons, coyotes, and skunks.
4. It means to have good understanding of things and good judgment.
5. "I don't care!"
6. Answers will vary.

PAGE 45

1. Yes. The shell is attached to the turtle's body.
2. A reptile.
3. Because most turtles move slowly on land.
4. A tortoise is a kind of turtle that lives only on land. There are about 50 species of tortoises.
5. Both animals have shells in which they can hide. Both also live in and out of water. Some crabs, though, can leave their shells.
6. Answers will vary.

PAGE 46

1. It means to attack suddenly.
2. Sample answers: Lions, cheetahs, leopards, and jaguars.
3. Sample answers: Giraffes, zebras, leopards, snakes, skunks, and dalmatian dogs.
4. Sample answers: Fingerprints, snowflakes, and every human being.
5. No. A cow doesn't have a pattern or color that blends in with its surroundings.
6. To hide in a forest, you would wear clothes in shades of green and brown. To hide in snow, you would wear white clothes.

PAGE 47

1. No. Different types of fish swim in different formations.
2. Because sharks are predators and don't need the protection of a group.
3. A group of lions is called a *pride*. A group of wolves is called a *pack*. A group of birds is called a *flock*.

4. Because if the person became tired or got a muscle cramp, he or she might drown if there were no one there to help.

5–6. Answers will vary.

PAGE 48

1. Both become inflated, or expand, when filled with air.
2. An amphibian. Amphibians live part of their lives in water and part on land.
3. A toad.
4. Into your lungs.
5. It means that you're having trouble speaking clearly, as though there were something stuck in your throat. Coughing helps to clear up the "froggy" sound so that you can speak clearly again.
6. To a place where there is water, such as a pond, a swamp, or a lake.

PAGE 49

1. Sample answers: Hares, kangaroos, frogs, toads, and grasshoppers.
2. 50 feet.
3. Sample answers: Carrots; leafy green plants, such as lettuce, grass, and weeds; twigs; and tree bark.
4. Answers will vary.
5. Sample answers: Bugs Bunny, Peter Rabbit, Peter Cottontail, Thumper, and Roger Rabbit.
6. Sample answers: By shouting a warning, pulling an alarm, blowing a whistle, setting up flares, putting up a warning sign, and flashing lights.

PAGES 50–51

1. A dam is a type of wall. A lodge is a home where beavers live.
2. So that they can gnaw through wood and cut down trees.
3. Because they spend a lot of time in the water building and repairing dams and lodges.
4. It means to work very hard and get lots of things done.
5. Canada.
6. Since a dam stops a stream from flowing, it prevents water from getting to people and plants farther down the stream that may need it.

One Step Further: The unwrapped jar will cool down the fastest. The wrapped jar in the box will stay the warmest because it has a lot of *insulation*, or layers of material, around it. A beaver's thick fur also acts as insulation to keep it warm.

PAGE 52

1. Its long, sticky tongue can go into small holes and attach itself to insects, which the woodpecker then pulls out and eats.
2. In a hole inside the trunk of a tree.
3. It holds on to the bark of a tree with its claws.
4. Sample answers: Squirrels, chipmunks, some kinds of monkeys, and koalas.
5. Sample answers: Week, weed, door, poor, deep, peek, keep, row, cow, crow, crowd, crop, core, dock, deck, and powder.
6. Sample answers: Anteaters, roadrunners, and grasshoppers.

PAGE 53

1. Because sharks sometimes attack people in the water. Rest of answer will vary.
2. Sharks lose many teeth in their lifetime and some of them get washed up on beaches.
3. A lost baby tooth will eventually be replaced by a permanent tooth.
4. A lost permanent tooth is not replaced and there is a gap in the mouth where the tooth was. A dentist can fill in the gap with an artificial, or fake, tooth.
5. Brush your teeth regularly, floss your teeth, see a dentist every six months, and avoid eating too much candy and other sweet foods.
6. Sample answers: Seats in a theater, crops in a field, and cars in a parking lot.

PAGE 54

1. It carries its baby on its back.
2. A joey.
3. Answers will vary.
4. Australia is southeast of Asia, in the southern hemisphere.
5. Sample answers: Kangaroos, wallabies, wombats, dingoes, kookaburras, Tasmanian devils, emus, and echidnas.
6. Answers will vary.

PAGE 55

1. People can move their lower jaw up and down, side to side, and forward and back.
2. Because it swallows its food whole, without chewing it.

3–4. Answers will vary.

5. Because the food could get stuck in the person's throat, block breathing, and cause choking.
6. The winding river looks similar to the shape of a snake.

PAGE 56

1. The openings in our nose through which we breathe air in and out.
2. So the hippo can breathe.

3–4. Answers will vary.

5. Because the night air is cooler than the air during the day.
6. An elephant and a rhinoceros.

PAGE 57

1. At night.
2. Sample answers: Our eyelids, a yellow caution traffic light, and the turn signal on a car.
3. Because the flashing light from a firefly looks like tiny flashes of lightning.
4. Both flash a light on and off to send a signal.
5. Sample answers: Fireplace, firewood, fireman, fireproof, firecracker, firehouse, and campfire.
6. Answers will vary.

PAGE 58

1. Eight (four on each foot).
2. Sample answers: Geese, swans, beavers, otters, and penguins.
3. To turn left, it would paddle only with its right foot. To turn right, it would paddle only with its left foot. Ducks also use their tails to help them steer.
4. Because its legs are set far back on its body. A duck does not have good balance on land.
5. Because flippers are wide and flat, like a duck's feet. They allow divers to swim through the water with more speed and power.
6. Because people are land animals. Our feet are designed so that we can move easily on solid ground.

PAGE 59

1–2. Answers will vary.

3. The suckers help an octopus move along the ocean floor, hold on to rocks, and catch food.
4. Both animals squirt liquids to protect themselves from enemies.
5. It means that the people separate and go in different directions, until the crowd no longer exists.
6. Answers will vary.

Other

books that will help develop your child's gifts and talents

Workbooks:
- Reading (4–6) $4.95
- Reading Book Two (4–6) $4.95
- Math (4–6) $4.95
- Math Book Two (4–6) $4.95
- Language Arts (4–6) $4.95
- Puzzles & Games for
  Reading and Math (4–6) $4.95
- Puzzles & Games for
  Reading and Math Book Two (4–6) $4.95
- Puzzles & Games for
  Critical and Creative Thinking (4–6) $4.95
- Phonics (4–6) $4.95
- Phonics Puzzles & Games (4–6) $4.95
- Math Puzzles & Games (4–6) $4.95
- Reading Puzzles & Games (4–6) $4.95
- Reading (6–8) $4.95
- Reading Book Two (6–8) $4.95
- Math (6–8) $4.95
- Math Book Two (6–8) $4.95
- Language Arts (6–8) $4.95
- Puzzles & Games for
  Reading and Math (6–8) $4.95
- Puzzles & Games for
  Reading and Math Book Two (6–8) $4.95
- Puzzles & Games for
  Critical and Creative Thinking (6–8) $4.95
- Phonics (6–8) $4.95
- Phonics Puzzles & Games (6–8) $4.95
- Math Puzzles & Games (6–8) $4.95
- Reading Puzzles & Games (6–8) $4.95
- Reading Comprehension (6–8) $4.95
- Reading Comprehension Book Two (6–8) $4.95

Story Starters:
- My First Stories (6–8) $5.95
- Stories About Me (6–8) $5.95
- Stories About Animals (6–8) $4.95

For Preschoolers:
- Alphabet Workbook $5.95
- Counting Workbook $5.95
- Word Workbook $5.95
- Animals Workbook $5.95

Reference Workbooks:
- Word Book (4–6) $4.95
- Almanac (6–8) $3.95
- Atlas (6–8) $3.95
- Dictionary (6–8) $3.95

Reference Book:
- Animal Almanac (6–8) $6.95

Science Workbooks:
- The Human Body (4–6) $5.95
- Animals (4–6) $5.95
- The Earth (4–6) $5.95
- The Ocean (4–6) $5.95
- Dinosaurs (6–8) $5.95

Science Book:
- Science Experiments (6–8) $5.95

Question & Answer Books:
- The Gifted & Talented® Question &
  Answer Book for Ages 4–6 $5.95
- Gifted & Talented® More Questions &
  Answers for Ages 4–6 $5.95
- Gifted & Talented® Still More
  Questions & Answers for
  Ages 4–6 $5.95
- The Gifted & Talented® Question &
  Answer Book for Ages 6–8 $5.95
- Gifted & Talented® More Questions &
  Answers for Ages 6–8 $5.95
- Gifted & Talented® Still More
  Questions & Answers for
  Ages 6–8 $5.95
- Gifted & Talented® Science Questions &
  Answers: The Human Body
  for Ages 6–8 $5.95
- Gifted & Talented® Science Questions &
  Answers: Animals
  for Ages 6–8 $5.95

For orders, call 1-800-323-4900.